Qui Beginners

Introduction

I want to thank you and congratulate you for downloading the book, *"Quilting for Beginners."*

This book is a quilting guide for beginners covering different quilting practices and techniques that you can use to come up with impressive quilt tops. If you have a growing passion or interest in quilting, this is the perfect book for you. Being a very practical activity, this book offers step by step practical lessons to enable you to have hands-on experience in the craft.

What fabrics are best for quilting? How do you go about quilt construction? What is batting? These are some of the questions, which will be explored throughout this book.

This book contains an introduction to quilting and a history of the craft, details on fabric for quilting, thread, batting, and tools together with quilt construction. It then goes on to highlight three projects for practical purposes. These include a "quilt as you go table runner," Easy Fence Rail Quilt and The Double Four Patch Baby Quilt. All these should be more than sufficient to get you started on your quilting journey!

Get ready for an amazing read full of the all the tips and tricks for quilting beginners.

Thanks again for downloading this book, I hope you enjoy it!

Table of Contents

Introduction

Chapter 1: Make Your First Quilt Today

Chapter 2: Brief History of Quilting

Chapter 3: Fabric for Quilting

1. Quilter's Weight Cotton

2. Home Décor Weight Cotton

3. Voile

4. Essex Linen

5. Quilter's Linen

Chapter 4: Thread, Battle and Tools

Chapter 5: Quilt Construction

Preparing your supplies

Making the blocks

Piecing the quilt together

Rotary Cutting

Piecing

Backing and Basting the Quilt

Quilting the Layers

Building the Quilt

Chapter 6: Project 1 Quilt as you go table runner

Chapter 7: Project 2 Easy Rail Fence Quilt

Chapter 8: Project 3 Double Four-Patch baby quilt

Thank you again for downloading this book!

Thank you and good luck!

References

Chapter 1: Make Your First Quilt Today

This book contains comprehensive information on how you can begin the journey of becoming an expert quilter. It starts by giving you a historical perspective of the origins of quilting as a practice. It educates you on how this craft has developed over the years up to the present moment. Since quilting uses fabric as its main material, the book tries to give you the different types of fabrics that you can use in the quilting process. It introduces you to a wide range of fabrics and offers suggestions on the best type of fabrics to use for your quilting project.

The book also introduces you to the tools that are required for quilting including the type of work that they perform. It gives descriptions of tools such as thread, batting, rotary cutter and many others which are essential for quilting. It also explains in detail how quilts are constructed and gives you a step by step explanation of the various stages of quilt construction. These stages include rotary cutting, piecing, backing and basting among others.

The book presents three quilting projects and gives an explanation of how the quilts are constructed. The first project is the quilt as you go table runner, which is usually designed for tables. The book gives a step by step explanation on how you can construct this quilt without encountering any problems.

The second project is known as the Easy Rail Fence Quilt, which is a simple quilting project that involves the use of strips and blocks. This type of quilting is described in a few simple steps. The book also offers the dos and don'ts associated with this quilting method.

Finally, the third project is the double four patch baby quilt project. The book provides insightful information on how you can construct this type of quilt by using quilting techniques that make the work easier and faster. This quilt is simple to construct only when you follow the instruction that this book provides.

Chapter 2: Brief History of Quilting

Quilts are known for their significance in homes due to their importance in performing a variety of purposes such as decoration, education, commemoration, bedding, and even artistic expressions. This is a craft familiar to many people and has a long history that is characterized by tradition. The term quilt originates from the Latin word *Culcita* which also means "stuffed sack." The exact origins of quilting still remain unknown even though the craft can be traced back to circa 3400 BCE to ancient Egyptians. It was introduced in Europe in the 11th century by Middle East crusaders. Quilted clothing became a household norm in the middle ages especially among knights who wore them under their armor. The "Tristan quilt" is known to be the earliest surviving quilt bed, which was designed in circa 1360 in Sicily.

Quilts later became popular in America in the 18th and 19th century. Quilts were widely used to provide warmth for colonists during winter. They were widely used because it was difficult to get new clothing and also it required a lot of labor to make homemade garments. Most quilts were made using salvaged fabrics which made the craft an effective way of cutting costs and maximizing resources. The practice was communal in nature where whole villages came together to engage in "quilting bees." This involved the practice where a group of people joined hands to make the same quilt. This practice was important in daily life - more so to women who were required to make a certain number of quilt items.

During the Industrial Revolution, manufactured clothing became more accessible. It was during this era that the sewing machine was invented. This is an important quilting tool that made quilting a much easier craft to practice. The sewing machine was made more accessible to people when the Singer

Company introduced an installment plan that made it possible for ordinary people to purchase it. With the emergence of the sewing machine, it was now possible for many women to devote their time to making quilts. This practice then became commercial and was no longer a domestic craft. This is because it took less time to make quilts. This led to a drastic change in the way quilts were traditionally made. The sewing machine, coupled with the existence of a wide range of colorful calicos, greatly transformed the quilting craft.

The most popular quilting style before the invention of the sewing machine was block-shaped. However, with the new technology, this trend suddenly shifted and people started to adopt a new type of quilts that was known as "crazy quilts." These types of quilts were made from different types of random and abstract shapes that were sewn together and embellished with embroidery. However, the story does not end there because the popularity of this craft still continues to the present time. In the recent past, the practice has experienced resurgence with the advent of seamstresses and DIYers. The history of quilting cannot only be based on American history, but it was also traditional in other countries as well. Other countries with a rich history of quilting include Bangladesh, Japan, West Bengal, West India, and Pakistan.

Chapter 3: Fabric for Quilting

There is a wide variety of fabrics with different textures and weights, which are used for quilting. It is usually difficult for beginners to know the best fabric to use for quilting. Here is a list of the most common fabrics used in quilting to help a beginner decide on the best choice of fabric to use and tips on how to choose the best fabric for quilting.

1. Quilter's Weight Cotton

This is a high-quality fabric that contains 100% cotton that is perfect to use for quilting. It is regarded as the best fabric to use for quilting. Normally, this fabric does not experience shrinkage. It is known to shrink less than most cotton fabrics that are cheap. Cotton fabrics that are of high quality bleed less often. It is advisable to test all fabrics for colorfastness when you need them for quilting. You can mostly find this type of high-quality fabric from quilt shops. Recently, there has been an emergence of national fabric chains that are now offering a wide range of quilting weight cotton fabrics from their stock. This type of quilting fabric is also used by many quilters and dressmakers as a form of clothing. This type of clothing should always be washed and dried before starting to cut or sew it to avoid shrinkage and issues related to fit after the garment is ready for use.

2. Home Décor Weight Cotton

This type of fabric is heavier than Quilter's Weight Cotton that features a sateen finish. It is highly suitable for quilted home décor. Due to its heaviness, this fabric does not drape well. However, it is an excellent fabric to use for quilted pillows, quilted bags, and throw cushions. It has a standard width of 54 inches, which is perfect for big home decor projects. This makes it highly economical. It can also be used for quilting but will require light batting due to its heaviness.

3. Voile

This type of cotton fabric is slightly transparent, silky, soft and light. Due to its lightweight nature, it is usually used for clothing such as dresses, blouses, scarves, and skirts. However, in the recent past, it has emerged to become one of the most preferred fabrics for quilting. Many quilters use it to design mix and match items with other quilting weight cotton. All voile fabrics, including a combination with other quilting weight cotton, can be used to construct quilts. It gives a softer and silky finish when used as a backing with quilting weight cotton.

4. Essex Linen

This is a natural fiber fabric created by Robert Kaufmann that is a blend containing 45% cotton and 55% linen. It has a good texture that can be combined with other quilting weight cotton. It is a good choice for sewing home decor and quilts.

5. Quilter's Linen

This type of linen was also created by Robert Kaufmann, which is an all-cotton fabric that looks, and feels like real linen. Most quilters use this fabric with other quilting weight cotton because it does not present problems that arise when mixing different types of fabrics. It is an excellent choice for sewing home décor and for quilting.

Chapter 4: Thread, Battle and Tools

Quilting uses different types of tools, which can sometimes become overwhelming. There are certain types of tools that are absolutely necessary for quilting whereas others can be put on a wish list for later use. If you are a beginner, there are some tools, which are considered to be "must haves." Such tools as a needle, a pair of scissors and thread are absolutely necessary for quilting. However, some tools have been designed to make work much easier. All your quilting tools can be found in your local quilting shop, local craft store, BERNINA store, or from an online retailer. Here are the most common tools for quilting.

1. Thread

There is a wide range of threads that can be used for quilting. However, the most important thing is to select the right type of thread for your project and machine. It is good to choose high-quality threads with less lint over bargain threads. It is important to note that thicker threads have a lower weight number. The lower the weight number, the thicker the thread, and vice versa.

2. Just like thread, there is also a wide variety of batting which ranges from thick to thin, polyester, wool, to cotton and so on. Batting comes with swatch cards, which will help you to select the right batting for your home project. You can find batting from any local quilt shop in your vicinity.

3. Fabric

You need to select the best fabric for your quilting project. This depends on the type of quilting project you wish to undertake – be it for building your hideout or making patterns. The type of fabric you use shows your creativity and expression. Use fabric that is 100% cotton for maximum effect. There are also other types of fabrics used for quilting such as satins, linen, silk and others.

4. Batting
There are different types of batting on the market. You have a choice of thick batting, thin batting, cotton batting, wool batting, and many others.

5. Cutting tools
The most common cutting tools used in quilting include rotary cutters and scissors. There are different brands and styles of rotary cutters. The blades of all rotary cutters soon wear out after much use. Therefore, you need to buy replacement blades for those that have gone blunt. Any quilter will agree that fresh blades are highly effective in performing cutting tasks. Fabric scissors are also crucial in any quilting project. These scissors should only be used to cut fabric and not be used for paper. Cutting paper with these scissors makes the blades dull quickly. You should try and have a smaller pair of scissors as well as a bigger pair.

6. Quilting ruler
This type of ruler comes in all shapes and sizes. Beginners should try to have a small square of about 5.5 inches-6.5 inches, and a long rectangle of about 6 inches x 24 inches. There are also other square and rectangular sizes to choose from.

7. Cutting Mat
Cutting mats, which are self-healing, are appropriate to use with your quilting ruler and rotary cutter on the fabric. Cutting mats come in different sizes ranging from pocket-sized mats to table-sized ones. Some cutting mats rotate and spin while some fold easily to allow for travel or storage. You can use an

18 inches x 24 inches cutting mat on your sewing machine and a 24 inches x 36 inches cutting mat on your cutting table.

8. Sewing tools
There are different types of sewing tools, which are used for quilting. Some of these tools include;

- Pins and clips
- Seam ripper
- Needles for a sewing machine and for hand stitching
- Sewing machine
- Oil and brush

9. Marking tools
These are tools that are used to mark the fabric. Some of these tools include;

- A water-soluble marker
- A chalk marking tool
- Clover marking tool

9. Assembly tools
You also need assembly tools to do a good quilting job. Some of the most common assembly tools include;

- Spray or basting pins
- Quilting gloves
- Iron
- Starch

10. Extras
These are tools, which are not necessarily needed in quilting but do come in handy sometimes. You might want to have such tools as;

- A pincushion
- A ruler holder or grip
- A specialty quilting ruler
- Extra feet
- A lamp
- A light box for tracing designs
- Color cards
- Design Wall
- Sewing machine travel case
- Sewing machine cover
- Die cutter for cutting complex designs

Chapter 5: Quilt Construction

The elementary quilting construction technique remains the same regardless of the quilting pattern that you use. Quilt construction follows three simple steps. These steps include;

Preparing your supplies

Such preparation includes activities such as selection of fabrics and cutting the pieces that you require for quilting. Quilting becomes faster when you have all your pieces cut and ready.

Making the blocks

Most quilts are constructed from blocks. You might have the same blocks, different blocks, or several sets of blocks. Each block consists of several pieces that should be joined together. When constructing a quilt it is good to always start at the center or with small pieces. You should lay out the pieces to help you have an idea of where to start piecing your blocks. It is good to join the smaller pieces first to form larger pieces to build the entire block.

Piecing the quilt together

The process of piecing the quilt together is similar to that of making your blocks but on a larger scale. You start by laying down all your pieces down to have a general idea of how your quilt will look like. Quilts that require sashing need sashing to join the blocks whereas those that do not require sashing should be joined directly to each other. You can personalize your finishing touches once you finish constructing your quilt top. You might want to make your quilt larger by adding borders to it.

Rotary Cutting

You start your quilting project with lots of small pieces. The first thing to do is cutting your fabric. This job is best done by a rotary cutter. In the past, when quilting was done by hand, quilters used scissors to cut the fabric. However, cutting fabric with a rotary cutter is much easier and faster, and more accurate than using scissors. Using a rotary cutter is difficult for beginners, but it gets much easier with time. It is recommended that you observe safety first when using this tool because you can easily injure yourself if you are not careful.

The best fabric to use for quilting is cotton. In case you are using cotton, it is good to preshrink, press, and starch it before rotary cutting. You should make this process compulsory if you are to get positive results. This is because most fabrics can be easily and accurately cut when they are crisp and properly prepared.

There are several tools that you need to do the rotary cutting. There are also a number of rotary cutters, which are available depending on the thickness or type of fabric to be used. You also need to have a template, a quilt ruler, and a cutting mat. The more variety of tools that you have the more options you will have. You need a rotary cutter that has a protective shield to avoid the occurrence of accidents when the cutter is not in use. The cutting mat works closely with the rotary cutter. Small cutting mats are suitable for small items while larger ones are good for multiple uses.

A good quilt ruler is one that has a non-skid surface or one that comes with a lip on the edge. Rulers that can slide easily are not effective when it comes to accuracy. You should understand the meanings of all the markings on the ruler to use it effectively. Templates and specialty rulers are optional but very useful to experienced quilters who are more skilled in the quilting practice. These tools are available in all shapes and sizes. Some of them have been made to do specific tasks like cutting applique pieces. Others are designed for specific types of quilt blocks or for custom quilt patterns.

Piecing

Special skills are needed to sew patchwork pieces into blocks, which are then assembled to form a quilt. This process is the same as putting a puzzle. Each piece has to fit perfectly to bring out the bigger picture. Patchwork piecing has several major goals - precision being one of them. You should be able to cut pieces that are precise so that they can fit together accurately. The other goal involves maintaining an accurate ¼ inch seam allowance, maintaining the flatness of the fabric by pressing, and lining up sewn seams well.

Patchwork pieces are usually sewn using straight stitches. However, it is advisable to use a smaller stitch length because the pieces you are using as well as the seam length are also small in size. It is not advisable to do backstitching when doing piecing. This is because you will still need to sew across the seam again as you continue building the block. The stitch width also needs to be adjusted. Adjusting the width on a straight stitch means that you move the switch to the right or left inside the oval opening of the needle plate. This measurement is less than a quarter inch.

The main reason why this technique is used is when two sewn pieces are ironed part of the quarter inch seam allowance is taken up in the fold of the ironed seam. The scant seam compensates for the loss and gives a more accurate matching and piecing of seams. This type of seam is used by more experienced quilters who construct complex quilts. The seam allowance accuracy is crucial if you want the pieces to fit together perfectly. It is always good to test your stitch setting by using a scrap and then measuring the seam allowance with a ruler or seam gauge.

You also need to understand the feeding system of your sewing machine to prevent your fabric from getting caught under the needle plate when piecing. You can also use a "starter" fabric, which is used as a scrap to help preserve your fabric from damage. You should also have the ability to adjust the foot pressure on the sewing machine. Foot pressure is a feature on your sewing machine, which is useful in accomplishing several tasks. Pressure can be modified depending on the thickness of the fabric when piecing. Light fabrics need more pressure while heavier ones require less. The foot pressure is also responsible for helping the machine to stitch evenly.

It is good to keep tabs on your blocks and the overall quilt layout before you start to piece them together. This will help you to work systematically following a certain method. You should be careful when putting pieces or blocks together to avoid sewing them out of order. You can use a design wall or place them on a cutting mat, or on a table near your machine. You have to pay close attention to the order to avoid confusion. Pressing the fabric is important in the piecing process. You should pay attention to the direction in which you press the seams of your pieces because it significantly contributes to how well your seams will line up as your construct your quilt top.

Backing and Basting the Quilt

To construct a quilt top you need to do a "quilt sandwich" by joining the batting and backing. First and foremost, you require a backing for your quilt. It is good to start creating simpler quilt backs that are still attractive enough. You can do this by using your favorite large scale print, adding a few simple stripes, or make use of orphan blocks from other projects, or from your current project. You can also use plain backing if you feel a little bit overwhelmed. Your quilt should be bigger than the front because some shifting of the layers occurs during quilting. Extra spacing should be added on the length and breadth of the quilt when making the backing.

After creating the top and the back we still need to do the middle or batting. It is advisable to use cotton batting for this task. Your batting should be bigger than the quilt top but smaller than your batting. The layers are then attached together using basting pins or spray basting. The backing should be laid on a flat side the wrong side up. It should then be taped at the corners and at an interval of every 6-8 inches. The backing should be stretched a little as you continue taping it. The batting is then laid on top and smoothed out. The quilt top is then laid on top of this with the right side up. The three layers are then pinned together at an interval of 3-4 inches apart. Start from the center and continue working out to the edges.

Quilting the Layers

The process of quilting the layers is guided by the fabrics and the seams. The three layers of the quilt can be combined using different methods. However, basting is the most important step in the quilting process. It seems to be tedious and tiring, but it brings out the best when done carefully. Basting is a temporary way of holding the three layers together while you do your quilting. Make sure that all the three layers do not have wrinkles and are also smooth. Press the backing fabric and lay it on the floor with the top facing down. Pull the fabric taut and tape it hard on the surface. Make the batting smooth and la the quilt top on top of the batting. Iron both layers to remove all the wrinkles. This helps ensures that the quilt top aligns itself to the batting.

You then roll both layers together. Unroll the quilt top and batting on top of the quilt back and smooth all the wrinkles. Make sure that you are able to see the backing fabric on all the four corners of the quilt top. Baste all the three layers together using spray baste or safety pins. Pin the quilt top starting from the center going outwards. Remove the tape after pinning it and make sure the back is flat and tight. If the fabric becomes loose, you will have problems with puckers and tucks when you start quilting. There will be no remedy for this problem when you start sewing. Holding the three layers together is functional and also creates visual interest and texture. The more you quilt to hold the three layers together with the longer it will last. It makes the fabric to last longer and the batting to shift less often.

Building the Quilt

Beginners find it difficult to build their first quilt. Some do not know where to start, what they need, and how to stitch the quilt together. If you are a beginner, it is good to choose a simple project and break it down into steps. You can make a good quilt by following these steps.

Step 1: Start with a small project to learn the basic techniques easily. You start by doing baby quilts.

Step 2: Gather all the materials and tools for the work. These will include the basic quilting and sewing tools. Choose the right type of fabric for your project including backing and binding fabric. To know how much fabric you require, try and find out the dimensions for your blocks to build the size of quilt that you want. You can also use a quilt fabric calculator to help you with the size.

Step 3: Cutting of the patchwork. In order to do accurate stitching of the patchwork, you need to cut it accurately.

Step 4: Sewing the patchwork. It is advisable to use a straight stitch seam to build a quilt top that will not be wavy or have puckers or unmatched seams. It is also good to sew your patchwork accurately for a perfect job.

Step 5: Joining together the quilt sandwich and basting all the three layers together. A well-basted quilt sandwich is less likely to have puckers or become distorted in the quilting process. You need a quilt fabric, a quilt batting, a large flat surface to work on during basting. You can use spray basting or pins to do basting.

Step 6: Quilting stitches. There are many methods that you can use to quilt the layers of the quilt sandwich. The most common quilting methods include free-motion quilting, straight line quilting, quoting with a general pattern, adhering to a patchwork design with quilting or building your own creative quilt.

Step 7: Binding the quilt. After quilting, it is important to add binding to make your quilt to have an impressive look. There are several binding methods, which you can use. It is good to find out which method best suits your needs.

Step 8: Appreciate your quilt. After finishing to build your quilt, it is good to label it so that you can remember when you made it and for what purpose. Sometimes you might want to make a quilt as a gift to someone. It is good to always enjoy and appreciate your work by making good use of it. You can even hang it on the wall and enjoy the fruits of your labor.

Chapter 6: Project 1 Quilt as you go table runner

Building the table quilted runner involves piercing and quilting simultaneously. The steps are as follows:

Step 1: The first step is deciding on the size of the table runner by using the table you are quilting to measure your batting piece. Remember to cut it bigger to compensate for shrinkage. Finally, cut the fabric while making it bigger at the corners than the batting.

Step 2: To stretch your batting, press under low heat while ensuring it doesn't go out of shape. Also, press the backing fabric the put the batting on the opposite side of the fabric. Flip the pieces and now press on high heat so that they hold together. Quilter's spray adhesive is also a good bonding alternative.

Step 3: For a variety of strips for the table runner, cut multiple, same length fabric strips and widths and arrange them over your backing and batting. Stack the strips from the center to make two piles on the left and right. On the first right side strip, sew a quarter an inch seam through the backing and batting.

Step 4: Open the seam, pin the left side strip and match them to the left edges. Sew a quarter an inch seam through the backing and batting. Repeat the steps, alternating the right and left piles until all the strips are sewn to the table runner corners.

Step 5: Start Quilting. You do this by starting from the middle and working towards the right side. You then come back to the middle again and work towards another direction. Sew a line down to the borders of the quilt/ place the foot parallel to the edge of your runner and drag your thread about an inch. Work with the foot again and sew a fresh row of quilting moving to the opposite direction. Square off the rough edges after finishing the process. You can then attach the binding.

Chapter 7: Project 2 Easy Rail Fence Quilt

A Rail Fence quilt is an easy project to undertake and even gives you a leeway to customize and personalize it. Each quilt block in this project consists of four segments that have been cut from strip-pieced fabrics. This makes it easy to do a yardage estimate.

Step1: Choose your size. You can use two way to choose the size of your rail fence quilt. You can use the finished block size of your quilt or the finished strip size. The most important consideration is to make it a rotary- friendly number. You can do this by rounding the size to an eighth of an inch.

Step 2: Choose your fabric. It is good to search for a light, medium or dark colored fabric for the project. This is because you can see the patterns better and this improves its attractiveness.

Step 3: Choose a pattern variation that you like. This type of quilt has many variations to choose from. However, they have something in common which is that they are all made of blocks, which are made of strips. This is a repeated pattern of strip squares. This construction uses the strip piecing technique. You can do this by cutting long strips of cloth at the desired measurement and sew them together to make a long ribbon that has many possibilities. Afterward, you whip out the strip and cut out shapes.

Step 4: Sewing. This is the bit where you do the quarter inch seam. You will have to sew many strips together. You should make sure you maintain the quarter inch seam allowance as you set your strips into blocks and the blocks into a quilt pattern. The seams should always be pressed towards the fabric.

Chapter 8: Project 3 Double Four-Patch baby quilt

Making a four patch baby quilt is an easy and simple process that can quickly be learned by a beginner. Here is how to go about it.

Step 1: Begin by using four squares of fabric of the same size. Take the squares on the left side and place them on top of those on the right side facing down. This means that the squares will be facing each other. This situation is known as "right sides together." If you have larger squares it is good to pin them together. Use a seam allowance of a quarter an inch and sew both sets of squares together with a straight stitch. Do not double stitch or backstitch as this can bring problems later.

Step 2: Put the sewn square on a presser without opening them. The seam allowance should ten be pressed with a hot iron. This ensures that the thread stays flat so that it maintains its flatness when the block is opened up and pressed.

Step 3: The pieces should be opened up and laid face down. Decide how you will press the seam allowance. It is good to press in opposite directions leading to the darker fabric. This helps to create a perfect intersection. Work slowly and carefully to avoid distorting the blocks.

Step 4: Put the right sides together again. This will make your seam allowance to face opposite directions. You can even notice when the blocks fall into place by using sliding your fingers to slide the blocks against each other.

Step 5: Pin the blocks. You can start pinning at the top, at the bottom, and at the intersection. You should also pin where you see additional space. You then sew using the seam allowance and remove the pins as work progress to sew.

Step 6: Lay the seam on an ironing board and then open up the block when it is facing the iron board. Push the seam allowance in different directions at the bottom and on top. This will make the middle stitches to loosen making them open up. Press it again flip it over and press it again. The end result is a perfect four patch block.

Conclusion

Thank you again for downloading this book!

I hope this book was able to help you understand how to quilt using the various materials and tools at your disposal. It is our hope that the book has helped you to understand the quilting practice and how you can use quilting techniques to come up with impressive quilt tops. The book had the intention of providing step by step practical lessons for the reader to enable him to have a hands-on experience in this craft.

Finally, if you enjoyed this book, then I would like to ask you for a favor, would you be kind enough to leave a review for this book on Amazon? It'd be greatly appreciated!

Thank you and good luck!

References

1. https://so-sew-easy.com/beginner-quilting-start/
2. https://feltmagnet.com/textiles-sewing/Common-Quilting-Mistakes-and-Tips-for-Beginners
3. http://sewdelicious.com.au/2012/09/quilting-for-beginners.html
4. https://www.craftsy.com/quilting/article/quilt-patterns-for-beginners/
5. http://www2.fiskars.com/Ideas-and-How-Tos/Crafting-and-Sewing/Quilting/How-to-Quilt
6. https://www.amexessentials.com/quilting-tips-for-beginners/

Manufactured by Amazon.ca
Bolton, ON